HN 29 .S724 1995 Vol.9

P9-CDH-376

The survey kit

DATE DUE

ILL RI8 1434676			
11.24.01			
NOV 2 3 2001			

DEMCO 38-297

NEW ENGLAND INSTITUTE
OF TECHNOLOGY
LEARNING RESOURCES CEN

THE SURVEY KIT

Purpose: The purposes of this 9-volume Kit are to enable readers to prepare and conduct surveys and become better users of survey results. Surveys are conducted to collect information by asking questions of people on the telephone, face-to-face, and by mail. The questions can be about attitudes, beliefs, and behavior as well as socioeconomic and health status. To do a good survey also means knowing how to ask questions, design the survey (research) project, sample respondents, collect reliable and valid information, and analyze and report the results. You also need to know how to plan and budget for your survey.

Users: The Kit is for students in undergraduate and graduate classes in the social and health sciences and for individuals in the public and private sectors who are responsible for conducting and using surveys. Its primary goal is to enable users to prepare surveys and collect data that are accurate and useful for primarily practical purposes. Sometimes, these practical purposes overlap the objectives of scientific research, and so survey researchers will also find the Kit useful.

Format of the Kit: All books in the series contain instructional objectives, exercises and answers, examples of surveys in use and illustrations of survey questions, guidelines for action, checklists of do's and don'ts, and annotated references.

Volumes in The Survey Kit:

1. **The Survey Handbook**
   Arlene Fink

2. **How to Ask Survey Questions**
   Arlene Fink

3. **How to Conduct Self-Administered and Mail Surveys**
   Linda B. Bourque and *Eve P. Fielder*

4. **How to Conduct Interviews by Telephone and in Person**
   James H. Frey and *Sabine Mertens Oishi*

5. **How to Design Surveys**
   Arlene Fink

6. **How to Sample in Surveys**
   Arlene Fink

7. **How to Measure Survey Reliability and Validity**
   Mark S. Litwin

8. **How to Analyze Survey Data**
   Arlene Fink

9. **How to Report on Surveys**
   Arlene Fink

THE SURVEY KIT

HOW TO
REPORT
ON SURVEYS

ARLENE FINK

SAGE Publications
International Educational and Professional Publisher
Thousand Oaks   London   New Delhi

10/99

32552393

Copyright © 1995 by Sage Publications, Inc.

All rights reserved. No part of this book may be reproduced or utilized in any form or by any means, electronic or mechanical, including photocopying, recording, or by any information storage and retrieval system, without permission in writing from the publisher.

For information address:

SAGE Publications, Inc.
2455 Teller Road
Thousand Oaks, California 91320
E-mail: order@sagepub.com

SAGE Publications Ltd.
6 Bonhill Street
London EC2A 4PU
United Kingdom

SAGE Publications India Pvt. Ltd.
M-32 Market
Greater Kailash I
New Delhi 110 048 India

Printed in the United States of America

Library of Congress Cataloging-in-Publication Data

Main entry under title:

The survey kit.
    p. cm.
    Includes bibliographical references.
    Contents: v. 1. The survey handbook / Arlene Fink — v. 2. How to ask survey questions / Arlene Fink — v. 3. How to conduct self-administered and mail surveys / Linda B. Bourque, Eve P. Fielder — v. 4. How to conduct interviews by telephone and in person / James H. Frey, Sabine Mertens Oishi — v. 5. How to design surveys / Arlene Fink — v. 6. How to sample in surveys / Arlene Fink — v. 7. How to measure survey reliability and validity / Mark S. Litwin — v. 8. How to analyze survey data / Arlene Fink — v. 9. How to report on surveys / Arlene Fink.
    ISBN 0-8039-7388-8 (pbk. : The survey kit : alk. paper)
    1. Social surveys. 2. Health surveys. I. Fink, Arlene.
HN29.S724   1995
300'.723—dc20   95-12712

This book is printed on acid-free paper.

99 10 9 8 7 6 5

Sage Production Editor: Diane S. Foster
Sage Copy Editor: Joyce Kuhn
Sage Typesetter: Janelle LeMaster

Contents

How to Report on Surveys: Learning Objectives

A survey's report consists of a summary and explanation of its findings, methods, and significance. Reports are of interest to the public, students in education and the social and health sciences, scientists and policymakers, and individuals in business and government and in the public and private sectors.

Surveys have a long history starting with the ancient Hebrews and Romans who used polls—one kind of survey—to collect census information for taxation purposes. In recent times, surveys have become one of the most popular methods of collecting data on nearly all of society's woes and wishes. Proper reporting of the results of these surveys is a skill that is almost comparable to composing a readable business letter or conveying information by telephone or electronic mail.

The aim of this book is to teach you the basic skills needed to prepare and interpret accurate and useful survey reports. Its specific objectives are to:

■ Prepare, interpret, and explain lists, pie charts, and bar and line charts

■ Prepare, interpret, and explain tables

■ Identify survey report contents for:

  – Oral presentations

  – Written presentations

  – Technical and academic audiences

  – General audiences

- Prepare slides

- Prepare transparencies

- Explain orally the contents and meaning of a slide or transparency

- Explain in writing the contents and meaning of a table or figure

- Explain orally and in writing the survey's objectives, design, sample, psychometric properties, results, and conclusions

- Review reports for readability

- Review reports for comprehensiveness and accuracy

1 Lists, Charts, and Tables: Presenting the Survey's Results

A survey's report can be written and/or oral and presented to large and small groups. The report's effectiveness and usefulness depend to a large extent on the clarity of its presentation. Lists, charts, and tables are used to maximize clarity.

AUTHOR'S NOTE: The names of all corporations and survey instruments used in examples throughout this chapter are fictitious.

1

Lists

Lists are used to state survey objectives, methods, and findings. The following examples of these uses of lists come from a formal talk about a survey of the use of mental health services in a large American city.

1. To State Survey Objectives

   Mental Health Services Questionnaire: Purposes

   TO FIND OUT ABOUT:

   - Accessibility
   - Satisfaction
   - Barriers to use

2. To Describe Survey Methods

   Seven Tasks

   - Perform literature review
   - Pose study questions
   - Set inclusion and exclusion criteria
   - Adapt the Prevention in Psychological (PIP) Function Survey
   - Pilot test and revise the PIP
   - Train interviewers
   - Administer the PIP

3. To Report Survey Results or Findings

PIP's Results

✓ **62% state that services are almost always inaccessible.**

   ▪ No difference between men and women

   ▪ No difference between younger and older respondents

✓ **32% of users are almost always satisfied.**

   ▪ Men more satisfied

   ▪ No difference between younger and older respondents

✓ **25% of potential users named at least one barrier to use.**

   ▪ Limited access to transportation most frequently cited barrier

═══════════════════════════════════════

Lists are simple to follow and so are very useful in survey reports. However, they typically need explanation in oral reports. One of the results illustrated in the example above is that no difference in satisfaction was found between younger and older respondents. The speaker must explain "younger" and "older" to the audience as these terms can vary from person to person.

Other terms, like inclusion and exclusion criteria (also in List 2), may need explanation. In written reports, lists can be used as a "table." For example, a report might use the second list above and precede it with a statement like "Table X lists the seven tasks that were needed to complete this survey of mental health use in an urban American city."

The following guidelines are helpful if you use lists in a survey report.

Guidelines for Using Lists in Survey Reports

1. *Use only a few words to express each idea.* Use short words, phrases, or sentences.

   Poor

   ### The Literature Review

   We conducted a review of the literature to find out about the barriers to use of mental health services by low-income residents of U.S. inner cities.

   Better

   ### The Literature Review

   Purpose: Identify barriers to use of mental health services

   Focus: Low-income residents of U.S. inner cities

2. *Be consistent.* Each part of the list should be just words, just phrases, or just sentences. Use the same part of speech to start. Use the same capitalization and punctuation in all lists.

Poor

One year's experience

Interviewers must be willing to drive within inner cities to conduct interviews in respondents' places of residence.

Better

- One year's experience
- Willing to drive within inner cities
- Willing to conduct interviews in respondents' residences

3. *Leave blank spaces between the elements of the list to make it easier to read.*

4. *Use marks (bullets, checks) to set apart elements of the list.* For example, bullets are used in the "better" example for Item 2.

5. *In a single presentation, keep the symbols consistent.* For example, use checks for main headings and bullets for secondary headings.

6. *Have no more than four items on the list in a slide and no more than eight in a handout.*

7. *Use colors and drawings sparingly and keep them consistent.* If you use blue for bullets and red for checks at the beginning of the report, stay with that color scheme until the end.

Pie Charts

A figure is a method of presenting data as a diagram or chart. Pie charts are one type of figure. They are used to show survey data as proportions, that is, percentages or numbers that are part of a whole. For example, you can use a pie chart to describe a survey's responses in percentages, as illustrated in Figure 1–1.

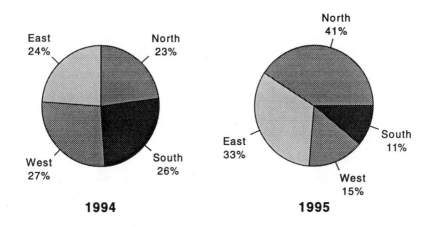

1994   **1995**

Figure 1–1.   City Responses: A Survey of Mental Health Service Use
SOURCE: Telephone interviews.

The pie chart is given a title and an explanation of the source of data—telephone interviews. As you can see from the pies, the response rates in all parts of the city were fairly equal proportionately in 1994 (ranging from 23% to 27%). In 1995, the northern part of the city substantially increased its responses, and the proportions throughout the city were no longer similar.

If you want to emphasize one "slice" of the pie, make it the darkest or lightest pattern or separate it from the rest. In Figure 1–2, the northern part of the city's increased response rate is emphasized by separation.

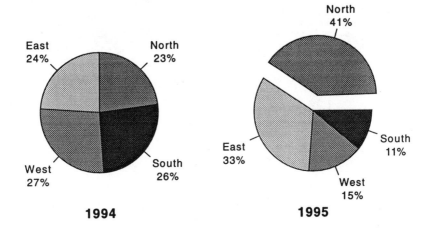

Figure 1–2. City Responses: A Survey of Mental Health Service Use
SOURCE: Telephone interviews.

To emphasize change in proportions, use two pies. If you want to show growth, make the second pie larger than the first. If you want to show decline, make the second pie smaller. In Figure 1–3, pies are used to show the impact after one year of a maternal and infant health program on costs of care for hourly workers at Smith and Zollowitz, Inc.

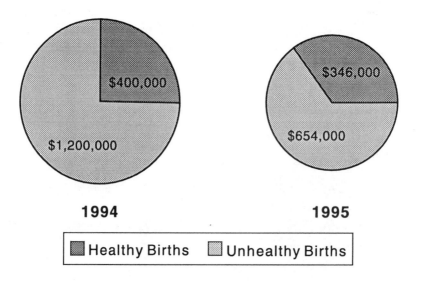

Figure 1–3.   Efficient Baby Care
SOURCE: Smith and Zollowitz, Inc. Reprinted with permission.

Looking at the two pies, you can conclude that the maternal and infant health program reduced the costs of caring for healthy and unhealthy births. The information in these pies comes from Smith and Zollowitz, Inc., and this is specified along with the statement that the pies are reprinted with permission. If data come from a source other than your own survey, you must put the origin directly on the figure. You have an ethical (and sometimes legal) obligation to name your source. Sometimes, you may have to request written permission to use copyrighted or proprietary information. The authors of the pie (or any other graphic illustration) will tell you exactly how they want to be acknowledged. Most U.S. federal government publications allow you to reprint data without receiving explicit permission to reprint. Of course, you are obligated to name the source of information. If in doubt, call the government agency directly.

The following guidelines are useful for the construction and use of pie charts.

Guidelines for Preparing Pie Charts

- Use pies to express proportions or percentages.

- Give the pie a relatively short title. Sometimes, a subtitle helps.

- Give the source of the data (e.g., telephone interviews or the ABC Company).

- Use no more than eight slices.

- If necessary, group the smallest slices together and label them "other."

- To emphasize a slice, separate it from the remainder of the pie or make it the darkest (or brightest) color or pattern.

- To emphasize changes over time, use larger pies to show growth and smaller ones to show shrinkage.

- Name the source of information for the pie. If the entire pie is reprinted from some other source, acknowledge it the way the authors want you to. Sometimes, you will have to get formal permission in writing to reprint the pie in your report.

WARNING

Do NOT use patterns on adjacent slices that create optical illusions.

Do NOT put red and green slices next to each other because about 5% of the population cannot distinguish red from green.

Bar and Line Charts

Bar charts (or graphs) depend on an *X*-axis and a *Y*-axis. The vertical axis is the *Y* and represents the unit of measurement or dependent variable, such as dollars, scores, or number of people responding. On the *X*-axis, you can put nearly all types of data, including names, years, time of day, and age. The *X*-axis usually has data on the independent variable.

Bar charts are often used in survey reports because they are relatively easy to read and interpret. Figure 1–4 shows the results of a 5-year study of curriculum preferences in five schools. Notice that the chart has a title, both the *X*-axis and the *Y*-axis are labeled, and the source of data is given.

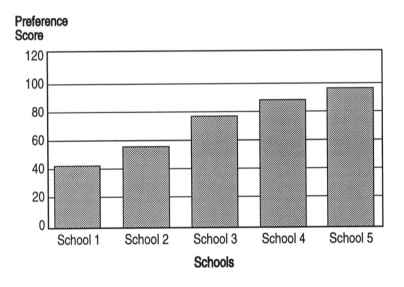

Figure 1–4. Curriculum Preferences in Five Schools
SOURCE: 1995 Curriculum Survey for Teachers.

The chart shows that Schools 1 and 5 appear different in their preference scores, with School 1 at just above 40 and School 5 at just under 100.

Bar charts can be used for many survey purposes, including comparing groups and studying changes over time. Figure 1–5 compares job satisfaction for clerical and technical workers over a 10-year period. Because two groups (clerical workers and technical workers) are involved, a key (or legend) to the meaning of the bars is given. Also, the company that sponsored the survey is named.

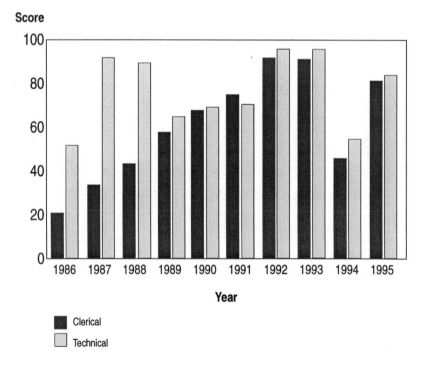

Figure 1–5. Job Satisfaction: A 10-Year Study
SOURCE: Satisfaction Inventory (higher scores are more positive).
NOTE: Study sponsored by the L. L. Green Company.

The chart shows that clerical workers' satisfaction has been lower than technical workers' for 9 of the 10 years. Only in 1991 were the positions reversed and clerical workers seemed more satisfied than technical workers.

You might complain that the use of 10 sets of bars clutters the chart. For more than six or seven bars, you can show the chart horizontally, as in Figure 1–6.

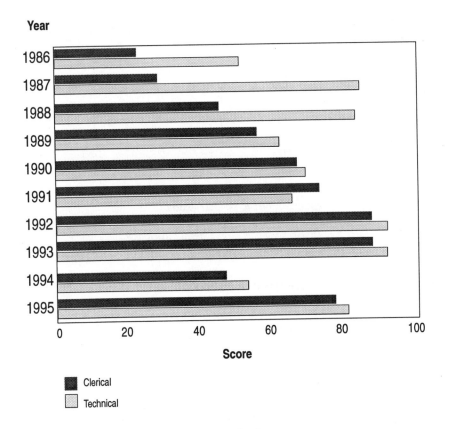

Figure 1–6. Job Satisfaction: A 10-Year Study
SOURCE: Satisfaction Inventory (higher scores are more positive).
NOTE: Study sponsored by the L. L. Green Company.

The same information can be presented in a line (Figure 1–7). Note also that to reduce the clutter, the years are grouped in units of two.

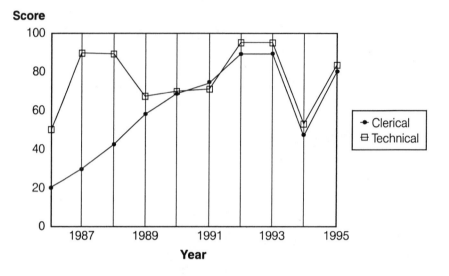

Figure 1–7. Job Satisfaction: A 10-Year Study
SOURCE: Satisfaction Inventory (higher scores are more positive).
NOTE: Study sponsored by the L. L. Green Company.

Keep bar and line charts simple. Use no more than four or five lines in any single chart.

Bar and line charts can be misleading, so be careful not to compromise your results. For example, 1,000 people were asked their opinions regarding use of national parks. The opinions were compiled into scores. Compare the report of opinions in June, July, and August on the next two bar charts (Figures 1–8 and 1-9).

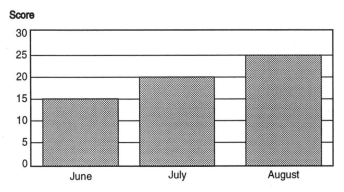

Figure 1–8. Opinion of National Park Reserves: A Survey of 1,000 Park Users SOURCE: Parks Department Annual Summer Questionnaire (high scores are most positive), U.S. Department of the Interior, Division of Parks and Land Management.

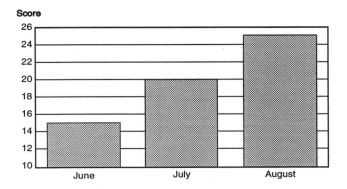

Figure 1–9. Opinion of National Park Reserves: A Survey of 1,000 Park Users SOURCE: Parks Department Annual Summer Questionnaire (high scores are most positive), U.S. Department of the Interior, Division of Parks and Land Management.

In Figure 1–8, the opinions do not *appear* to be as different from one another as they do in Figure 1–9, even though a close reading of the data show that the two contain identical scores. Two features of the charts change the purely visual interpretation. First, Figure 1–8 has a "zero" starting point; Figure 1–9 does not. Omitting the zero makes the change look greater than it is. If your chart does not start with zero, this should be indicated.

The second reason why the charts look different is that the values chosen for the Y-axis greatly affect the graphic presentation of data. Look at Figures 1–10 and 1–11.

Frequency

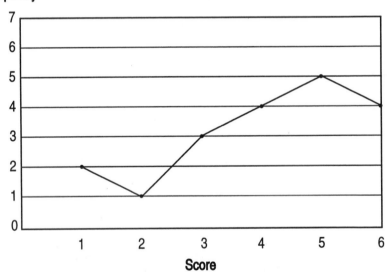

Score

Figure 1–10. Children and the Dress Code
SOURCE: Dress Up and Dress for Education (DUDE) Survey.
NOTE: Children were asked their opinion of a new dress code. The chart shows the number or frequency of children, with scores ranging from 1 to 6. Higher scores are more positive.

Frequency

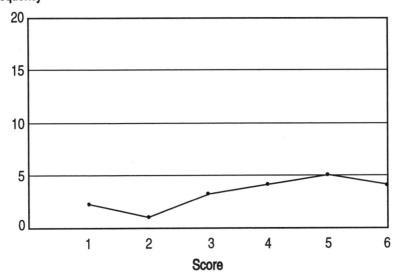

Figure 1–11. Children and the Dress Code
SOURCE: Dress Up and Dress for Education (DUDE) Survey.
NOTE: Children were asked their opinion of a new dress code. The chart shows the number or frequency of children, with scores ranging from 1 to 6. Higher scores are more positive.

Change appears less dramatic when the Y-axis has many points separating each value (in Figure 1–11, five points separate each frequency value) than it does when the Y-axis has few points (in Figure 1–10, one point separates each frequency value).

The magnitude of change can also be maximized or minimized by the choice of starting time. Look at Figures 1–12 and 1–13.

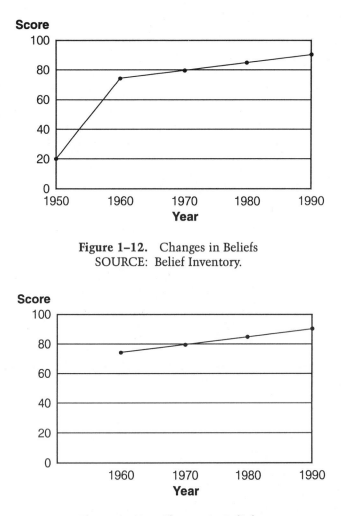

Figure 1–12. Changes in Beliefs
SOURCE: Belief Inventory.

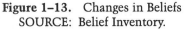

Figure 1–13. Changes in Beliefs
SOURCE: Belief Inventory.

Figure 1–12 shows that the biggest change in beliefs scores
occurred in 1950. Figure 1–13 does not show this; the scores
look fairly consistent over time.

> **WARNING**
>
> Use bar and line charts with caution. Be wary of differences that are made to appear important even if they are not. Many professional journals require that *apparent* differences be explained. Are they statistically significant? Do they have practical meaning?

Look at the next two illustrations. They represent the results of a survey comparing changes in eating, smoking, and dietary habits among students. Some of the students were in the Health Assessment and Prevention Program for Youth (HAPPY), and some were in a control health program. Figure 1–14 suggests that changes (for better and worse) took place for all behaviors, including whether or not students ate fast food and stopped smoking. Figure 1–15 explains the differences. Using statistical tests, the changes in smoking and exercise are not statistically significant (with $p < .05$ as the level of significance). Notice also that figures, when used in scholarly publications, place their associated explanations underneath.

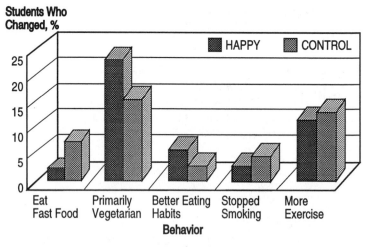

Figure 1-14.   HAPPY Versus Control
SOURCE: Health Assessment and Prevention Program for Youth.

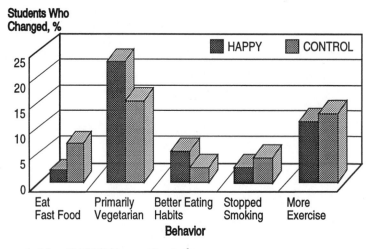

Figure 1-15.   HAPPY Versus Control
SOURCE: Health Assessment and Prevention Program for Youth.
NOTE: Health-promotion-related behavior changed from baseline to follow-up. Results of chi-square tests for each behavior were $p < .05$ for eating fast foods, for primarily vegetarian, and for better eating habits; $p < .10$ for stopped smoking; and $p < .60$ for more exercise.

A list of guidelines for constructing and using bar and line charts follows.

Guidelines for Preparing
Bar and Line Charts

- Give each chart a title.
- Explain the meaning of the values on the X-axis and Y-axis.
- Clarify the context of the survey. (For example, it was conducted at the XYZ Company.)
- Give the source of information.
- Use bar charts to compare groups or show changes over time. The bars should be vertical. If using more than six bars, consider a horizontal chart or use lines.
- Provide a key, or legend, to special shadings or types of lines, if more than one group or time period is depicted in a chart. For example, the key for the results of a survey of two groups might indicate that the results for Group 1 are represented by a dotted line and those for Group 2 by squares.
- Keep charts as uncluttered as possible. For example, instead of printing all years in a 10-year study, group them by twos. Use no more than four or five lines in a chart.
- Use line charts to compare survey results over many points in time.
- Choose the values for the Y-axis so that the results are accurate reflections of the survey's findings. If you do not start at zero, indicate this directly on the chart.
- Choose accurate starting times when illustrating change.
- Explain the meaning of the differences that appear on the chart. Are they statistically significant?
- Place explanations of the figure underneath it.

Tables

Tables are used to summarize data about respondents and their responses and to compare survey results over time. Suppose you are responsible for surveying students in an experiment to find out if their health habits can be improved through a teen-based program called the Health Assessment and Prevention Program for Youth (HAPPY). Students in three high schools are randomly assigned to HAPPY or a control health program. The survey's main objectives are to describe and compare the students in each program and to compare their health habits (e.g., willingness to exercise regularly) before entering the program, immediately after, and 2 years later. If you achieve the survey's objectives, you will produce tables that look like these "shells."

1. *Description of Students in HAPPY and the Control Program*

The table will contain the number (*n*) and percentage of the sample (%) in HAPPY and in the control program that are different ages (years), go to different high schools, are male or female, and speak primarily English, Russian, Spanish, or some other language at home.

Characteristics	HAPPY		Control	
	n	%	*n*	%
Age (years)				
Under 13				
13 - 15				
16 - 17				
Over 17				
High school				
Grant				
Lincoln				
Clinton				
Gender				
Female				
Male				
Primary language spoken at home				
English				
Russian				
Spanish				
Other (specify)				

→

2. *Changes Over Time in HAPPY and the Control Program: Willingness to Exercise Regularly*

The shell table below is set up to compare scores on a 25-question Exercise Inventory.

Timing	HAPPY Scores	Control Scores
Before HAPPY		
Immediately after		
Two years after		

When should tables be used? Tables are especially useful in written reports because the reader can spend time with them. Technically oriented people also like them in oral presentations. Actually, little information is available to conclusively guide you in the choice of charts versus tables. If you need to make a visual impact, then charts are appropriate. If you want to illustrate your points with numbers, then tables are appropriate. Often, survey reporters offer a variety of tables and charts in a single report.

The following guidelines are useful when preparing tables for survey reports.

Guidelines for Preparing Tables

- *Column headings are determined by the most important comparison.* For example, if you are comparing boys and girls to find out if age and city make a difference in their responses to a survey, you will have two main column headings: boys and girls.

If you are describing the characteristics (e.g., age or educational level) of users and nonusers of seat belts, the values (e.g., numbers and percentages of persons with the differing characteristics) go in the columns.

Characteristics	Users		Nonusers	
	n	%	*n*	%
Age (years)				
Under 18				
18 - 25				
26 - 35				
36 - 45				
46 and over				
Gender				
Male				
Female				

→

Characteristics	Users		Nonusers	
	n	%	n	%
Years using				
Less than 1				
1 - 3				
4 - 6				
Over 6				

- *If appropriate and possible, put statistical values in ascending (largest values) to descending order.* The table below describes the results of a nationwide survey of 734 people who were asked whether they preferred basketball or baseball.

Statistical Values in Order:
The National Sports Preferences Survey[a]

Region	Number of People Choosing		Total
	Baseball	Basketball	
Northeast	140	124	264
South	100	52*	152
West	89	138**	227
North Central	45	46	91
Total	374	360	734

a. Survey administered by the Center for Sports and Health, Washington, D.C.
*$p = .003$; **$p = .002$.

Note that in this table the preferences for baseball are in descending order. The choice of which values to place first depends on the points being emphasized. If the survey's focus was on preferences for basketball, then the first cell of the table under "Region" would have been West.

- *Use a standardized set of symbols to call the reader's attention to key aspects of the table, such as statistical significance.* For example, in the previous table, the superscript "a" comes first and tells you the source of data. The next two symbols (asterisks) tell you the p values, a statistic that helps you decide if the results you found in the survey are the consequence of a program or of chance. To find sets of symbols, check out the tables in journals that are appropriate to your field of study or interest.

Talking About the Survey

Learn About the Listeners

A typical concern of anyone who has to report on a survey is how simple or technical to be. The first task is to estimate the needs of the audience. In general, one of three scenarios is likely:

Scenario 1: The audience consists of nontechnical people. They want to know what the survey found, if the findings are important, and how to use them. They are not interested in the methodological details and in statistics and tables.

Scenario 2: The audience consists of technical people. They want details on the survey's methods. What was the response rate? How was the sample chosen? Were differences found in the demographic characteristics of respondents and nonrespondents?

Scenario 3: The audience is mixed. Some are interested in statistics and tables, and others are not.

How can the needs of all of the groups be met? The good news is that certain reporting principles apply to all audiences. These include the general topics that should be included in the talk and the need for simplicity and variation. The amount of time spent on various aspects of the talk and the depth of coverage varies. If you are unsure of the composition of the audience or you are fairly certain it is mixed, then prepare a relatively nontechnical talk and be prepared to augment it for the more technical types with a discussion period or with written handouts.

All talks are enhanced with visual aids. The most common are overhead transparencies and slides.

Overhead Transparencies and Slides

Overhead transparencies are acetate sheets onto which letters or figures have been transferred. They can be prepared by using water-soluble or permanent-ink felt-tip pens, photocopying typed or computer-generated materials, or generating direct copies from a laser printer. You need a special projector to use overheads. Slides are usually 35 mm (2-inch × 2-inch) and also need a special projector.

Both overheads and slides have advantages and disadvantages, as shown in the following table.

	Overheads	**Slides**
Advantages	Can be prepared quickly and economically	Compact: easily carried and stored
	Speaker faces audience, facilitating discussion	Suitable for any size audience
	Easy to carry and store	Projectors are readily available
	Uses ordinary room lighting	Tend to be considered "professional"
	Can make additions or deletions during the talk	
	Can change the order during the talk	
Disadvantages	Projectors are large and heavy	Relatively expensive
	Projectors may block the listeners' view of the screen	Need extra time for designing
	Can be messy if frequent erasures are made	Need extra time to process
	Mechanics of keeping overheads in focus may distract listeners	Need a really darkened room: inhibits discussion and note taking
		No changes of any sort possible during the talk

The following guidelines can assist when preparing overheads. Illustrations of transparencies in use are given in the next section, Talking About Surveys.

Guidelines for Preparing
Overhead Transparencies

- Each transparency should contain only one main idea, table, or figure. Complex transparencies force the listeners to focus on the overhead and not the talk or to give up on the overhead and listen to the talk.

- Use the 6 × 6 rule: 6 words per line and 6 lines per transparency.

- Limit yourself to about 7.5 × 9.5 inches on an 8.5-x-11-inch overhead.

- Use simple letter styles and fonts like Helvetica, Roman, and Courier. Letters should be about 3/8 inches high or 18-point type.

- Use upper- and lowercase letters.

- Colors are useful to emphasize a point, illustrate similarities and differences between points, and show the actual color of an object. Color can be added by using colored sheets (overlays) or felt-tip marking pens.

- Make sure that the projector does not block the listeners' view of the screen.

- Before you discuss a transparency, check the screen to make sure that the machine is focused and that the overhead is straight.

Use the following guidelines to prepare slides. Illustrations of slides in use are given in the next section, Talking About Surveys.

Guidelines for Preparing Slides

- Limit each slide to one main concept.

- Allow the listener 1 to 2 minutes per slide. The exception to this is when you have similar slides in a sequence, such as lists, pies, or graphs, or with the same format.

- If you adapt information from a textbook or other survey, check to see if it needs to be simplified.

- Prepare slides using the features of word processing or graphic programs. Special slide-preparation software can also be used.

- Use no more than 7 to 9 lines of text per slide and no more than 6 or 7 words per line.

- To emphasize points, underline titles, use bullets or check marks, number each point, or use contrasting colors to separate points.

- Use phrases, not complete sentences.

- Highlight key words by underlining, using different type size, alternative spacing, or different colors, or putting them in a circle or box.

- If you have "down time" with no appropriate slides, use a filler. These often consist of an opaque, blank slide or the title of the presentation. Do not use cartoons as the filler because they are distracting in the middle of a talk. (If you use cartoons to lighten the presentation, make sure the audience can see the caption.)

- Use handouts to summarize information and provide technical details and references. Make sure that your name, the name of the presentation, and the date are on each page of the handout. Do not distribute handouts until you are finished speaking *unless* you refer to them during your talk.

- In general, upper- and lowercase letters are easier to read than all uppercase.

- Round numbers to the nearest whole number. Try to avoid decimals, but if you must, round to the nearest tenth (32.6%, *not* 32.62%).

- Limit tables to 5 rows and 6 columns.

- If graphs are used, make sure that both the *X*- and the *Y*-axes are clearly labeled.

- Make sure that *all* information on the slide is discussed in the talk.

- The minimum height of the letters should be .5 mm. Use the largest letters possible to fill the area available.

- Use bold type.

- Use slides that have a blue or black background with white lettering.

- Use no more than four colors per slide.

- Avoid these color combinations: green, blue, and gray; black, blue, and brown; and white and yellow.

- Review the slides before you talk. Nothing is more embarrassing than misspelled words and upside-down slides. Place a mark or spot in the lower left corner of each slide mounting. When slides are in the projector, rotate each slide so that the mark is on the outer right edge facing you. You should load the slide tray yourself to make sure you have all the slides you need in the order you want them.

Talking About Surveys: Step by Step

When talking about a survey, remember the preacher's proverb:

> First, you tell 'em what you're gonna tell 'em, then you tell 'em, then you tell 'em what you told 'em, and then you tell 'em what to do with it.

What *you're gonna tell* is the introduction, *telling* is the methods and results, *what you told* is the conclusion, and *what to do* are the implications, recommendations, or next steps.

TALKS AND TITLES

The title should be brief and understandable to listeners and clearly limit the topic. Phrases like "a report of," "an analysis of," or "the use of" should be avoided because they add words but do not clarify much.

Poor

> An Analysis of a Survey of Boys' and Girls' Attitudes to the New Dress Code

> A Report of a Survey of Boys' and Girls' Attitudes to the New Dress Code

Better

> Boys' and Girls' Attitudes to the New Dress Code

Poor

> The Use of a Survey in Comparing Boys' and Girls'
> Attitudes toward the New Dress Code

Better

> Comparing Boys' and Girls' Attitudes toward the New
> Dress Code

Alternative

> Attitudes toward the New Dress Code: Comparing Boys
> and Girls

The talk should include the names of persons who made sufficiently large contributions to the survey's purposes, methods, and write-up so that if called upon, they too could report on it (even if they would need some assistance to do so). In some cases, you are ethically (and legally) bound to mention who sponsored (paid for) the survey. You may also want to include the geographic location of the report and the date. The following are sample slides showing authors and acknowledgments.

Authors (slide)

> **ARE WE SATISFIED**
> **WITH OUR WORK?**
>
> **A COMPARISON OF FULL-TIME**
> **AND PART-TIME EMPLOYEES**
>
> **Prepared by the Work Study Team**
>
> **Presented by Martin Federman**
>
> **Los Angeles, California**

Acknowledgments (slide)

> **ACKNOWLEDGMENTS**
>
> **Technical Foundation**
>
> **Work and Leisure Corporation**

HOW TO INTRODUCE THE TALK

The introduction should point out the purposes of the talk and address the topics that will be covered or the questions that will be answered. It helps also to tell the listener the order that your talk will follow. The following are two slides showing a presentation's purposes and questions and an overhead with the talk's order.

Purposes of the Talk (slide)

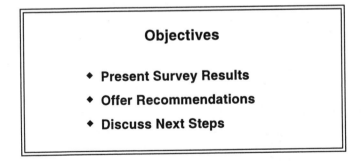

> **Objectives**
>
> ◆ **Present Survey Results**
> ◆ **Offer Recommendations**
> ◆ **Discuss Next Steps**

Questions Answered by the Talk (slide)

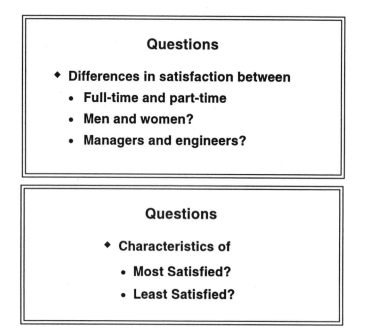

Order of the Talk (transparency)

What to Expect

♦ **Background: Why Survey Satisfaction**

♦ **Who Participated**

♦ **How Chosen**

♦ **The Survey: Contents and Statistical Properties**

♦ **Findings**

♦ **Conclusions and Recommendations**

The introduction to an oral presentation also consists of the information you think listeners should have to put the survey in its proper context. The background can include some or all of the following:

1. *Why the survey was done.* What is the problem or issue that the survey's data are supposed to help resolve?

2. *The setting in which it takes place.* The setting includes the political, social, and educational environment. Survey information can be used to help describe current status, monitor changes, and recommend future programs and policies. For example, if a survey has been conducted to help management decide how to reorganize a department, your presentation will discuss the current organization and review the issues pertaining to reorganization that the survey is specifically designed to help resolve.

3. *Unique features.* A survey can be unique in many ways. It may be the first of its kind in the organization, the first to involve the participation of certain members of an organization, or the first to reach a special group of respondents. Also, the findings may be unusual: either going against the conventional wisdom ("We all thought we would find that . . . ") or going against the findings of other surveys and studies ("A survey of children's feelings about strict dress codes directly contradicts our results. . . ").

The introduction to a talk is especially challenging because you can lose or win the audience during it. To encourage listening, several techniques are advocated:

Ask a question that will be answered during the presentation. For example, for a talk on work satisfaction, you might ask the audience "Do you think younger and older employees differ in their satisfaction?" "What about the bosses? How satisfied are they, do you think?"

Make a controversial statement that will be supported by the survey's findings. For example, you might say, "A number of studies have shown that more generous maternity leave policies are associated with greater work satisfaction, but we did not find this to be true."

Relate the survey's topic or findings to a current event.

Tell a relevant personal experience.

Tell a humorous anecdote related to the topic of the survey.

Refer to a previous talk or to its topic.

OVERVIEW OF THE SURVEY

Provide a brief overview of the survey to focus the listeners and help them get a feeling for its size and scope. Concentrate on the following:

- *Type of survey* (telephone or face-to-face interviews, mailed or self-administered questionnaires, reviews of records, observations, or other)
- *Number of participants and response rate* (Example: "More than 100 people participated, giving us about 86% of all who were eligible.")
- *How long the survey took* (Example: "We conducted 15-minute interviews over a 6-month period.")
- *Survey's general contents* (Example: "Of the 50 questions, nearly all asked about satisfaction with work, although about 10 focused on demographic questions like age and income.")

Think of the overview as part of the introduction. That is, you are providing the context for the survey. Later on in your talk, you will go into greater detail about the contents and responses.

Next, tell the audience the specific characteristics and contents of the survey. You will probably want to illustrate one or more questions.

Characteristics (slide)

> ## Survey Characteristics
>
> * **25 Questions**
> * **Mailed Questionnaire**
> * **One Follow-up Mailing**
> * **$10 per Each Completed Survey**

Content (slide)

> ## Survey Content
>
> * **5 Questions: Mental Health**
> * **5 Questions: Physical Health**
> * **10 Questions: Social Functioning**
> * **5 Questions: Demographic**

Sample Question (transparency)

**Sample Question:
Social Functioning**

During the past month, how often did you feel iso-
lated from others?

                                    (Circle One)

Always	1
Very often	2
Fairly often	3
Sometimes	4
Almost never	5
Never	6

TALKING ABOUT PSYCHOMETRICS

Psychometrics is a branch of measure development that
deals with the design, administration, and interpretation of
quantitative assessments. Some surveys are designed to quantitatively assess constructs. In measurement language, a construct is a relatively abstract variable as contrasted with a
variable that is operationalized in terms of measurable or
quantifiable indicators. Depression is an example of a mental
health construct. You can operationalize it by asking a series
of questions linked to depression and including inability to
sleep, mood, frequency of crying, feelings of isolation, and so
on. The questions asked in the survey define or operationalize

the construct. But does the survey consistently distinguish among people who are depressed and those who are not? If it does, it is valid (and reliable). When a survey claims to measure depression, or any other construct for that matter, its reliability and validity must be quantitatively demonstrated.

Reliability refers to the consistency of a score and the extent to which a measure is free from random error. Validity means the extent to which a measure measures what it is supposed to and does not measure what it is not supposed to. A scale is an aggregation of one or more questions ("items") that cluster together and can be scored as one measure. Sometimes, a survey has several scales. For example, a survey of health might use scales for physical health and for emotional health. A score on one scale is independent of a score on the other (for a more complete discussion on surveys and psychometrics, see **How to Measure Survey Reliability and Validity,** Vol. 7 in this series).

To describe the key psychometric properties of a survey—reliability, for example—a transparency might be appropriate.

Scenario: Facing Each Act With Resolve (FEAR) is a self-administered questionnaire to measure ability to cope with natural disasters like floods, fires, and earthquakes. FEAR has three scales: Concern, Coping, and Satisfaction With Coping. Internal consistency reliability is calculated. This is a method for estimating score reliability from the correlations among the items in the scale. Coefficient alpha is an internal consistency reliability coefficient.

The following transparency is prepared.

Internal Consistency Reliability Coefficient (N = 300)

Scale	No. Items	Mean	Reliability Coefficient
Concern	10	73	.92
Coping	2	93	.71
Satisfaction With Coping	1	61	.63

HIGH SCORES MEAN MORE CONCERN AND BETTER COPING AND SATISFACTION

Highest Score = 100 Points

When you have a transparency or slide that contains a table, **you must explain the title, the headings, and any other contextual or organizing information** before you describe the data in the table and, when appropriate, offer interpretations. You must not assume that the audience can routinely read tables, much less read yours.

Listen in on the following report.

EXPLAINING A TABLE

Explain the title. "The next slide gives the internal consistency reliability coefficients for the FEAR questionnaire. The coefficients were computed based on the scores of 300 respondents."

Explain the headings. "The first column contains the three FEAR scales [points to the appropriate place on the screen]:

Concern, Coping, and Satisfaction With Coping. The next column contains the mean score [points to the appropriate place on the screen]. The third column contains the reliability coefficient for each scale [points to the appropriate place on the screen]."

Explain any other information necessary for the listener to follow the talk. "High scores are the most positive, with the highest possible score on all scales being 100 points."

Explain the contents of the table. "As you can see, the Concern Scale has 10 items, with a mean score of 73. Reliability is .92. Coping has 2 items, with a mean score of 93 and a reliability coefficient of .71. Satisfaction With Coping has 1 item, a mean of 61, and a reliability of .63."

Interpretation. "We concluded that the internal consistency reliability coefficients were sufficiently high for our purposes."

TALKING ABOUT DESIGN

A design is a way of arranging the environment in which a survey takes place. The environment consists of the individuals or groups of people, places, activities, or objects that are to be surveyed.

Some designs are relatively simple. A fairly uncomplicated survey might consist of a 10-minute interview on Wednesday with 50 parents to find out if they support the school bond issue, and if so, why. This survey provides a cross-sectional portrait of one group's opinions at a particular time, and its design is called cross-sectional.

More complicated survey designs use environmental arrangements that are experiments, relying on two or more groups of participants or observations. When the views of randomly constituted groups of 50 parents each are compared, the survey design is experimental.

Experimental designs are characterized by arranging to compare two or more groups, at least one of which is experimental. The other is a control (or comparison) group. An experimental group is given a new or untested, innovative program, intervention, or treatment. The control is given an alternative. A group is any collective unit. Sometimes, the unit is made up of individuals (e.g., men who have had surgery, children who are in a reading program, or victims of violence). At other times, the unit is self-contained (e.g., a classroom, company, or hospital).

Two types of experimental designs are commonly used. The first is called a concurrent control design in which participants are randomly assigned to groups. Concurrent means that each group is assembled at the same time. For example, when 10 of 20 schools are randomly assigned to an experimental group while at the same time 10 are assigned to a control, you have a randomized controlled trial, or true experiment.

A second type of experimental design uses concurrent controls, but the participants are *not* randomly assigned. These designs are called nonrandomized controlled trials, quasi-experiments, or nonequivalent controls.

Other experimental designs include the use of self-controls, historical controls, and combinations. Self-control survey designs require premeasures and postmeasures and are called longitudinal or before-after designs. Historical controls make use of data collected from participants in other surveys. Combinations can consist of concurrent controls with or without pre- and postmeasures.

A second category of survey design is descriptive (sometimes called observational). These designs produce information on groups and phenomena that already exist. No new groups are created. A very common descriptive design is the cross-section.

Cross-sections provide descriptive data at one fixed point in time. A survey of American voters' current choices is a cross-sectional survey. Cohorts are forward-looking designs that provide data about changes in a specific population. Suppose a survey of the aspirations of athletes participating in the 1996 Olympics is done in 1996, 2000, and 2004. This is a cohort design, and the cohort is 1996 Olympians. Case controls are retrospective studies that go back in time to help explain a current phenomenon. At least two groups are needed. Suppose you survey the medical records of a group of smokers and of a group of nonsmokers of the same age, health, and socioeconomic status and then compare the results. This is a case-control design. A design is internally valid if it is free from nonrandom error or bias. A study design must be internally valid to be externally valid and to produce accurate findings (for more about survey design, see **How to Design Surveys,** Vol. 5 in this series).

When making oral presentations, you may want to visually explain the design. One relatively simple way to do this is to use the "organization chart" function of a computer graphics program.

Consider the following example of the hypothetical use of a survey entitled FEAR, which measures ability to cope with natural disasters like fires, floods, and earthquakes. People are eligible to join a program to combat their fears (Program Combat) or a control group if they are over 18 years of age, are willing to attend all 10 group sessions, and can converse comfortably in English. The control consists of a 1-hour film. The design is an experimental one using concurrent controls without randomization because participants choose which of the two (the program or the control) is more convenient and likely to be more effective for them.

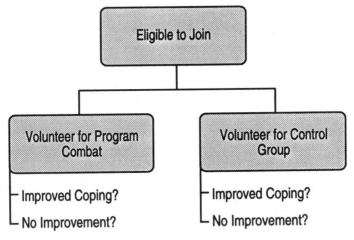

Figure 2-1.   Coping With Catastrophe: The FEAR Survey Design

When you present the audience with a figure (including pie, bar, and line graphs), you must explain it. You cannot assume that the audience will automatically comprehend it. Listen to this explanation:

> The FEAR survey design is an experimental design. Specifically, it uses concurrent controls without randomizing participants. The very top box [point, if appropriate] represents all participants who were eligible for the experimental or control groups. You probably recall that to be eligible, people had to be over 18, willing to attend 10 sessions, and comfortable speaking English. Participants could choose which of the two aspects of the experiment they preferred. This is shown in the diagram [point, if appropriate]. At the conclusion of the experiment, we surveyed everyone in both groups and compared whether they perceived that their abilities to cope had improved or not. This is shown on the third level of the diagram [point, if appropriate]. As you can see, neither group improves.

TALKING ABOUT SAMPLING

A sample is a portion or subset of a larger group called a population. Surveys often use samples rather than populations. A good sample is a miniature version of the population— just like it, only smaller. The best sample is representative or a model of the population. A sample is representative of the population if important characteristics (e.g., age, gender, health status) are distributed similarly in both groups. Suppose the population of interest consists of 150 people, 50% of whom are male, with 45% over 65 years of age. A representative sample will have fewer people, say, 75, but it must also consist of 50% males, with 45% over 65.

Survey samples are not meaningful in themselves. Their importance lies in the accuracy with which they represent or mirror the target population. The target population consists of the institutions, persons, problems, and systems to which or whom the survey's findings are to be applied or generalized.

The criteria for inclusion into a survey consist of the characteristics of individuals that make them eligible for participation; the exclusion criteria consist of characteristics that rule out certain people. You apply the inclusion and exclusion criteria to the target population. Once you remove from the target population all those who fail to meet the inclusion criteria and all those who succeed in meeting the exclusion criteria, you are left with a study population consisting of people who are eligible to participate.

How large should a sample be? The size of the sample refers to the number of units that needs to be surveyed to get precise and reliable findings. The units can be people (e.g., men and women over and under 45 years of age), places (e.g., counties, hospitals, schools), and things (e.g., medical or school records).

The most sensible way to produce the right sample size is to use statistical calculations. These can be relatively complex, depending on the needs of the survey. Some surveys have just one sample, and others have several (for a more complete discussion, see **How to Sample in Surveys,** Vol. 6 in this series).

In an oral talk, you should consider providing a description of the inclusion and exclusion or eligibility criteria, the sampling method or design, and the sample size, as illustrated in the following two survey scenarios.

> *Scenario 1:* This is a handout for a report of the inclusion and exclusion criteria used in a survey to find out which is most effective in getting adults to stop smoking: nicotine gum alone, nicotine gum and a support group, or a support group alone.

ELIGIBILITY

Target Population: **Patients who smoke**

Inclusion Criteria:

- **Between the ages of 18 and 64 years**
- **Smoke one or more cigarettes daily**
- **Alveolar breath CO determination of more than eight parts per million**

Exclusion Criterion:

- **Any contraindications for nicotine gum**

Scenario 2: These are two transparencies to report on sample selection and size in a survey of high school students who participated in a project to favorably modify their acquired immunodeficiency syndrome (AIDS)-related knowledge and beliefs. For the survey, schools were paired so that one urban and one suburban high school were joined. High schools A and C are urban; B and D are suburban.

HOW SAMPLE WAS CHOSEN

	Experimental		Control	
	AB	CD	AB	CD
Schools	AB	CD	AB	CD
Grade	9	11	11	9
% Sample	30%	30%	20%	20%
# Classrooms	16	13	13	10
# Students	430	309	326	251

SAMPLE SIZE

	Experimental	Control
Classrooms	29	23
Students	739	577

EXERCISE

Suppose you are asked to describe the contents of the preceding two transparencies ("How Sample Was Chosen" and "Sample Size"). Write out the talk you will give.

■ **SUGGESTED ANSWER** ■

The first transparency shows how the sample was chosen from four schools. The four were divided into two pairs: Schools A and B were one pair, and C and D were the second. Both pairs participated in the experimental and control groups, but as you will see, if the 9th grade was in the experimental group, the 11th grade in that pair was in the control. (Point to the screen.)

The table shows you the schools, the grade in each school, the percentage sample of that grade, the number of classrooms, and the number of students.

Ninth- and 11th-grade students participated. If 9th-grade students were in the experimental group in Schools AB, then 11th-grade students were in the control in CD. A 30% sample was taken of all experimental grades as was a 20% sample of the control. (Point to the screen.)

The next slide shows the total sample size of classrooms and students. As you can see, 29 classrooms were involved in the experimental group and 23 in the control group. This means 739 students were involved in the experimental group and 577 in the control group.

TALKING ABOUT DATA ANALYSIS

Surveys produce observations in the form of narrations or numbers. The narrations consist of responses stated in the survey participant's own words. Narrations are counted, compared, and interpreted, often using methods borrowed from communications theory and anthropology.

Survey data also take numerical form. For example, in some surveys, respondents may be asked to rate items on ordered or ranked scales, say, with 1 representing a very positive feeling and 5 representing a very negative one. In other surveys, they may be asked to tell their age, height, or number of trips they have taken or books they have read. The analysis of numbers or observations that take numerical form is done using "statistics." The results of statistical analyses are descriptions, relationships, comparisons, and predictions, and these are the most common types of analyses done for surveys.

Reporting the analysis methods and the results of the analysis often provide the greatest challenge in an oral report. Differences exist in the amount of detail that you can present in a written report and in a visual aid. In a written report, you are often expected to provide detailed tables and figures. In an oral report, the detail cannot be on the visual aid. You must verbalize it with or without the help of a handout.

The following tables are examples of the same data, dangers in the home, presented in two ways: as an in-text table for a written report and as a handout or slide for an oral report.

For a Written Report

	% Experimental Homes[a]	% Control Homes[a]	p[b]	Adjusted Odds Ratio	95% CI[c]
Living room					
Rugs (tripping danger)	22.5	35.2			
Peeling paint	10.6	14.5			
Floor in need of repair	4.9	3.7			
Any problems	28.5	40.2	< .001	0.55	0.45, 0.68

$\rightarrow$

	% Experimental Homes[a]	% Control Homes[a]	p[b]	Adjusted Odds Ratio	95% CI[c]
Hall					
Rugs (tripping danger)	9.3	15.8			
Peeling paint	4.3	10.2			
Floor in need of repair	2.4	2.0			
Any problems	13.0	20.1	< .001	0.54	0.41, 0.71
Bedroom					
Rugs (tripping danger)	12.2	14.7			
Peeling paint	6.8	9.2			
Floor in need of repair	3.1	2.1			
Any problems	16.9	17.8	.02	0.73	0.55, 0.95
Kitchen					
Rugs (tripping danger)	16.2	16.0			
Peeling paint	10.6	11.3			
Floor in need of repair	7.8	3.5			
Any problems	25.5	21.3	.24	1.15	0.91, 1.45

a. Percentages are based on the evaluation of 902 homes in the experiment and 1,060 in the control.
b. Logistic regression adjusted for the presence of children 5 years of age and younger and adults over 70 years of age.
c. CI = confidence interval.

For an Oral Report (either handout or slide)

	E, %	C, %
DANGER IN THE HOME:		
902 Experimental and 1,060 Controls		
Living Room	28.5	40.2*
Hall	13.0	20.1*
Bedroom	16.0	17.8
Kitchen	26.5	21.3
*p < .001		

The table for the written report contains three more columns than does the one for the oral report. Also, the table in the written report contains more detailed information comparing specific dangers (rugs, peeling paint, floor in need of repair) in each room. The essential information is in both tables: the comparison groups (experimental and control), the size of each group, and whether or not the differences between groups are statistically significant. A statistically significant difference between groups suggests that differences are likely to be the result of participation in the experiment rather than a chance finding. You can also use the table for the written report as a handout. (More information on how to do and interpret statistical analyses for surveys is found in **How to Analyze Survey Data,** Vol. 8 in this series.)

The Written Report

A useful written report provides enough clearly explained information so that at least two interested individuals can agree on the survey's objectives, methods, and conclusion. If the report is being submitted to a funding agency, such as the government or a foundation, the composition and format may be set for you. In most situations, you are on your own in deciding what to include and how long the report should be. The following is a checklist of the contents to consider in preparing the report.

Checklist of Contents for a Survey Report

✓ **List the title, authors, sponsors, location of report, and date.**

Make sure the report has a brief, clear title. Tell who prepared the report. If appropriate, distinguish between preparation of the report and conduct of the survey. Specify the sponsor of the survey: Who asked for it? Who paid for it? In what town, city, state, or province was the report written? What is the date of the report?

✓ **In the introduction, state the need or problem to be solved and the research questions to be answered or hypotheses to be tested.**

✓ **List the survey's characteristics.**

- *Type of survey instrument(s)* (e.g., mailed self-administered questionnaire, face-to-face-interview, observation, record review, telephone interview). Tell why the particular type was chosen. For example, was the survey available and previously validated? Were interviews more appropriate than self-administered questionnaires? Why?

- *Contents*

  Number of questions

  Description of content of questions

  Descriptions of response types (e.g., ratings from 1 to 5, with 1 = *most positive* and 5 = *most negative*)

  Description of scales (e.g., Attitude Toward Academics is a 20-question survey with two different scales of 10 questions each; one scale surveys attitudes toward school and the other measures attitudes toward reading)

■ *Psychometric characteristics*

Scales

— Content

— How questions are scored

— How questions are combined into scales

Reliability

— How established (stability, equivalence, homogeneity, and inter- and intrarater)

— Adequacy of reliability for survey's uses

— Adequacy of description and methods for establishing reliability

Validity

— How established (content, face, criterion, construct, convergent)

— Adequacy of validity for survey's uses

— Adequacy of description and methods for establishing validity

■ *Administration and other logistics*

Characteristics of survey administrators (e.g., education, experience)

Description of training activities for interviewers and other data collectors

Characteristics of quality assurance methods to ensure that survey is administered and interpreted in a uniform way by everyone who administers it

Length of time to complete each survey

Length of time for entire survey to be completed

- *Relevant literature and other surveys on the same topics*

✓ **Explain the survey methods.**

- *Design*

  Experimental or descriptive

  Limits on internal and external validity

- *Sample*

  If a population, explain

  If a sample, how selected (probability sample or convenience sample)

  If more than one group, how assigned

  How sample size was chosen

  Potential biases (e.g., because of how sample was chosen or assigned, sample size, and missing data from some or all respondents on some or all survey questions)

- *Analysis*

✓ **Relate results to the survey's objectives, research, or study question.**

✓ **State conclusions.**

- Summary of important points

- How findings compare to other surveys (yours and surveys done elsewhere)

✓ **State implications (meaning) and recommendations (next steps).**

Academic and Technical Survey Reports

Basically, two types of survey reports are the most common. The first consists of the academic survey report. This is a report prepared for specific rather than general audiences. The audiences can be in universities, business, and government, and the expectation is that a great deal of technical detail will accompany the results and recommendations. Below are two illustrations of what, for the sake of convenience, are called academic or technical survey reports.

Illustration 1: The Competencies of Generalist Physicians

A national survey is conducted of a representative sample of program directors and faculty in academic medicine who are pediatricians, general internists, and geriatricians. The survey is designed to find out the most important competencies for generalist physicians to acquire and sustain in medical school, as residents, and 7 years into their practice. The results will be used in guiding curriculum development policy.

Illustration 2: Drug-Exposed Babies

The state commissioned a survey of 56 county welfare service agencies to learn about the caseload and nature and quality of services given to drug-exposed babies. The report was prepared by the Statistics Branch of the Welfare Agency and will be used to devise a minimal data set and also as a basis for making decisions regarding welfare services in the state.

Survey Reports for General Audiences

The second type of survey report is designed to reach a general audience. Do not mistake "general" for "not too bright."

General audiences may consist of the public in general, but they may also contain people who can run businesses, schools, and government. You should assume that a general audience is very smart but not an expert in the specific topic covered by the survey. Examples of reports for general audiences are given below.

Illustration 1: Drug-Exposed Babies
A report of a survey of the state's welfare services for newborns exposed to drugs is given to both branches of the legislature and to the press.

Illustration 2: Satisfied Employees
A report of a survey of employee satisfaction is given to the company's Board of Directors and to all employees.

Illustration 3: Quality of Life of College Seniors at Technical University (TU)
A report of a survey given to all college seniors is written for the Office of Student Affairs at TU. It is available to all students and members of the faculty.

Contents of Reports

Technical reports or components of them often serve as the basis of reports for more general audiences. Because of this, they tend to be longer and more comprehensive. Also, their organization is usually different. In technical reports, the conclusions and recommendations are placed after the methods. In general survey reports, the main findings are almost always placed up front. Examples of tables of contents and lengths of each chapter are given in the following outline.

Table of Contents for a Technical Report

Executive Summary

Title page: Authors, geographic location of survey report, date

Acknowledgments: Sponsors of the survey; data collectors; participants; research, field, and technical assistance

Text of summary

The Report

Title page: Authors, geographic location of survey report, date

Acknowledgments: Sponsors of the survey; data collectors; participants; research, field, and technical assistance

Table of contents

List of tables

List of figures

1. *Introduction*—5 to 10 pages

   Need or problem to be solved

   How survey fits into the context of others previously done

   Survey objectives

   Research questions/hypotheses: Description of main outcomes and independent variables

   Limitations imposed by scope and focus of survey

   ■ Comment: Tell about the particular need or problem the survey's data will help resolve. Survey data are used to describe the current status and inform program development and policymaking. For example, a company might sponsor a survey of employees' satisfaction to find out how things stand now or to determine if new programs (such as work-at-home programs) or policies (such as a change in supervisory practices) are needed. If the survey is part of a research study, state the hypothesis or research questions. For which independent and dependent variables will the survey's data be used? What are the survey's specific purposes?

Keep the introduction relatively brief. Most readers want to quickly get into the body of the text. Save comments and background literature to help support your conclusions and recommendations. Tell the reader what the survey covers and excludes either here or later in the conclusions. For example, if the survey is about parents' attitudes, you might say something like this: "We interviewed parents in English and Spanish. We restricted the questions to attitudes toward the dress code and new library and counseling programs."

2. *The Survey*—20 pages

Type (e.g., interviews, mailed questionnaire)

Number of questions for entire survey and all subscales

Description of content

Administration: Time to administer, time to complete, duration of data collection

Relevant literature and other surveys

- Comment: The reader should have a clear idea of the characteristics of the survey: its type, length, contents, and time to complete. Give example questions. Make the entire survey form available to readers by listing in a table the questions and response formats, placing the survey in an appendix, or telling how it can be obtained. If appropriate, give the theoretical framework for the survey. Suppose the survey is about consumer preferences. Do the questions come from a psychological theory regarding how people make choices and take risks? Are some or all of the questions based on the work of others or other surveys? If so, describe and cite those sources.

3. *Design*—3 to 5 pages

   Description

   Justification

   Limitations and threats to internal and external validity

   ▪ Comment: Describe the design (experimental? descriptive?) Why was the design selected? Also, tell the design's impact on external and internal validity. (Limitations can be described here or later in the conclusions.)

4. *Sampling*—25 pages

   Inclusion and exclusion criteria

   Sampling methods: Description, explanation, and justification

   Sample size: Explanation and justification

   Potential biases resulting from sampling methods

   ▪ Comment: Describe who was eligible to participate and how they were selected (at random? by volunteering?). Justify the choice of method. How was the sample size arrived at? Did all who were eligible agree to participate? Did all who agreed also complete all survey questions? What biases are introduced into the survey's responses because of the nature of the sampling methods and sample? (You may prefer to answer this in the conclusions.) A bias is a systematic error that affects the accuracy and applicability of the survey's findings. For example, people who do not complete the entire survey may be different in important ways from those who do. They may be more verbal (perhaps more educated) or more motivated and interested in the survey topic.

5. *Psychometrics:* Reliability and Validity—1 paragraph to 20 pages

   Reliability: How ensured (including pretesting, training, and quality assurance activities) and how calculated

   Validity: How ensured and established

   ■ Comment: Many surveys are fairly simple and do not have sophisticated psychometric properties. For example, a 10-item questionnaire to find out customer preferences probably does not warrant the extensive psychometric validation that a survey of health status does. However, even short, relatively simple surveys should be administered in a standardized way with assurances that the respondents understand the questions and can provide reliable information. A one-paragraph description of reliability and validity can suffice for relatively simple surveys.

   Many surveys consist of many scales, all purporting to measure attitudes, values, and opinions. The data from these surveys are used to make important decisions that affect large numbers of people. For more complex surveys, it is very im- portant that information about reliability be provided. Not only do you want to prove that the data are reliable and valid, you must also demonstrate that you have used a high-quality method and described it adequately.

6. *Results*—15 pages

   Response rate

   Description of respondents

   Outcomes for each survey objective, research question, or hypothesis

   ■ Comment: The results or findings tell what the survey data suggest or show. For example, if you are comparing men and women at three points in time regarding their beliefs, as measured by the BELIEF Questionnaire, you will answer these questions:

1. What do men believe at Time 1? Time 2? Time 3?

2. Do men change significantly in their beliefs over time?

3. What do women believe at Time 1? Time 2? Time 3?

4. Do women change significantly in their beliefs over time?

5. How do the changes observed in men and women compare?

Do not interpret the results for the reader in this section. Just report the data that were obtained from the survey. Interpretation comes next—in the conclusions.

The following is an example of how to write up the results of survey data that have been analyzed statistically:

Table A contains data from a study of Program CAREER whose purpose is to prepare college students for entry into the job market. For the study, Program CAREER students are compared to other students who do not participate in a special program. Both groups, totaling 500 participants and nonparticipants, are surveyed before and after Program CAREER begins. To make the comparisons, scores are averaged for surveys of knowledge, beliefs, self-reliance, and risk-taking behaviors. The averages are tested for differences using a statistical method called a *t* test. In this case, the test is used to examine differences in the observed change score (after the program minus before) for each measure.

Table A
Before-and-After Mean Scores (standard deviations) and
Net Change Scores, by Program Group (N = 500 students)

| Survey Measures | Program CAREER Students | | No-Program Students | | | | |
	Before Program CAREER	After Program CAREER	Before Program CAREER	After Program CAREER	Net Difference	t	p
Knowledge	75.6 (11.8)	85.5 (8.8)	78.8 (10.9)	81.2 (9.6)	7.50	8.9	.0001*
Beliefs							
Goals	2.5 (1.1)	2.1 (1.0)	2.5 (1.1)	2.3 (1.1)	−0.15	1.5	.14
Benefits	3.5 (0.7)	3.8 (0.7)	3.7 (10.7)	3.8 (0.7)	0.19	4.7	.0001*
Barriers	4.4 (0.6)	4.5 (0.6)	4.4 (0.6)	4.4 (0.6)	0.09	1.2	.22
Values	5.4 (0.9)	5.5 (0.8)	5.5 (0.9)	5.5 (0.9)	0.09	0.7	.50
Standards	2.8 (0.6)	2.9 (0.6)	2.8 (0.6)	2.8 (0.6)	0.12	3.0	.003*
Self-reliance	3.7 (0.7)	3.9 (0.7)	3.7 (0.7)	3.8 (0.7)	0.10	2.2	.03*
Risk-taking behavior	1.5 (2.5)	1.3 (2.3)	1.0 (2.0)	1.3 (2.4)	−0.48	2.8	.006*

*Statistically significant.

More information on how to do and interpret statistical tests like the *t* test is found in **How to Analyze Survey Data, Vol. 8 in this series.**)

Before you write the results, answer these questions for yourself:

1. *What do the columns represent?* In this example, the columns give data on the mean scores and standard deviations (in parentheses) for CAREER and No-Program students before and after the program. The net difference in scores and the *t* statistic and *p* value are also shown. (**How to Analyze Survey Data** provides more information on the standard deviation, *t* statistic, and *p* values.)

2. *What do the rows represent?* In this case, the rows show the specific variables that are measured—for example, knowledge and goals.

3. *Are any data statistically or otherwise significant?* In this case, knowledge, benefits, self-reliance, and risk-taking behavior are statistically significant, as indicated by an asterisk. (To be significant, differences must be attributable to a planned intervention, such as Program CAREER, rather than to chance or historical occurrences, such as changes in vocational education that are unrelated to Program CAREER.) Statistical significance is often interpreted to mean a result that happens by chance less than once in 20 times, with a *p* value less than or equal to .05. A *p* value is the probability of obtaining the results of a statistical test by chance. (**How to Analyze Survey Data** provides more information on the meaning and uses of statistical significance.)

4. *Can these data stand alone?* In this example, you cannot tell because no other information is given. Sometimes, one table is compared to another or some of the data in one table are compared to another.

Here's how to write up the results.

> Table A presents the before-and-after means and the observed net change scores for each of the eight survey measures for the 500 Program CAREER and comparison students. Significant effects favoring Program CAREER were observed for five of the eight measures: knowledge, beliefs about benefits and standards, self-reliance, and risk-taking behaviors.

7. *Conclusions*—10 pages

What the results mean

Applicability of the results to other people and settings

- Comment: This is the place to summarize and interpret the results. Are they good? Bad? How do they fit into the context of other surveys? Do they support or contradict other people's findings? You can also discuss some or all of the limitations of the survey's design, sampling, scope, and focus. Remind the reader that your findings hold for the group that was surveyed but may or may not be applicable to other settings (e.g., offices, schools, towns).

8. *Recommendations*—10 pages

- Comment: Some surveys are conducted to provide data to decision makers or makers of policy who then determine what to do with the findings. In this situation, recommendations are not called for. When recommendations are required, be careful not to go beyond your survey or the findings. That is, be sure that if you recommend an activity you have evidence that it will work. Did the survey ask about the activity? Can you cite a reference that suggests that the activity is likely to be effective?

References

Appendixes
  The survey itself; additional technical information, including methods for selecting samples, determining sample size; complex or detailed statistics

Body of report: Maximum 115 pages

Table of Contents for a General Report

Executive Summary
  Title page: Authors, geographic location of survey report, date
  Acknowledgments: Sponsors of the survey; data collectors; participants; research, field, and technical assistance
  Text of summary

The Report
  Title page: Authors, sponsors, geographic location, date
  Acknowledgments: Sponsors of the survey; data collectors; participants; research, field, and technical assistance
  Table of contents
  List of tables
  List of figures

1. *Introduction*—2 pages
   Need or problem to be solved
   How survey fits into the context of others previously done
   Survey objectives
   Limitations imposed by scope and focus of survey

2. *Summary of Major Findings or Results*—10 pages

3. *Survey Content*—1 page

4. *Participation Rates*—1 page

5. *Other Methods: Administration, Reliability, and Validity*—
   1 page

6. *Conclusions and Recommendations*—10 pages

References

Appendix (Same as for the technical report; can make this a separate volume)

Body of report: 25 pages

A NOTE ON REPORT LENGTH

A report that is 300 pages long is unlikely to be read in its entirety. Sometimes, very long reports are prepared as documentation of the development and validation of important surveys, especially those that are used in research. Generally, though, reports need not be longer than 100 to 125 pages, and most can be 25 to 50.

THE EXECUTIVE SUMMARY

An executive summary provides all potential users with an easy-to-read report of the survey's major objectives, characteristics, findings, and recommendations. The summary usually varies in length from 3 to 15 pages. Executive summaries are often required and always advisable.

Three rules govern the preparation of the summary:

- Include only the most important objectives, characteristics, findings, and recommendations.
- Avoid jargon.

  Poor: We used a ***cluster sampling strategy*** in which schools were assigned at random . . .

  Better: We assigned schools at random . . .

  Poor: We established ***concurrent validity by correlating scores*** on Survey A with those on Survey B.

  Better: We examined the relationship between scores on Surveys A and B.

- Use active verbs.

  Poor: The use of health care services ***was found*** to be more frequent in people under 45 years of age.

  Better: The survey found more frequent use of services by people under 45 years of age.

  Poor: ***It is recommended*** that the FLEX Hours Work Program be implemented within the next 3 months.

  Better: We recommend the implementation of the FLEX Hours Work Program within 3 months.

Reviewing the Report for Readability

After writing a survey report, review it for readability. The conventional wisdom believes that most people are comfortable reading below their actual level. For general audiences, ease of reading is especially important. Here is one formula:

1. Take a 100-word sample of the survey report.
2. Compute the average number of words in each sentence. If the final sentence in your sample runs beyond 100 words, use the total number of words at the end of that sentence to compute the average.
3. Count the number of words in the 100-word sample with more than two syllables. Do not count proper nouns or three-syllable word forms ending in *-ed* or *-es*.
4. Add the average number of words per sentence to the number of words containing more than two syllables and multiply the sum by 0.4.

- ■ Example: Suppose a 100-word passage contains an average of 20 words per sentence and 10 words of more than two syllables. The sum of these is 30. Multiplying 30 by 0.4 gives you a score of 12. This means that the passage requires a 12th-grade reading level.

Reviewing the Report for Comprehensiveness and Accuracy

The following tabular "scoring" sheets are provided as a guide to the preparation and review of written and oral survey reports. All tables use the same scale:

$$4 = \text{Definitely yes}$$
$$3 = \text{Probably yes}$$
$$2 = \text{Probably no}$$
$$1 = \text{Definitely no}$$
$$0 = \text{No data; uncertain}$$
$$NA = \text{Not applicable}$$

INTRODUCTION AND BACKGROUND	4	3	2	1	0	NA
Are the survey's main objectives or guiding questions stated measurably?						
If the survey is part of a research study, are the research questions or hypotheses stated precisely?						
Is a description given of how the survey fits into the context of previous surveys done locally?						
Is a description given of how the survey fits into the context of previous surveys done elsewhere?						
Are the people or agencies that commissioned the survey acknowledged?						
Are the actual writers of the report acknowledged?						
Are the people or agencies responsible for conducting the survey acknowledged?						
Is an explanation provided of the problem or need the survey's data are to resolve?						
Other?						

SURVEY CONTENT	4	3	2	1	0	NA
Is the total number of questions given?						
Is the content of the survey adequately described?						
Is the number of questions given for each scale or subscale?						
Is the content described adequately for each scale?						
Are the response choices adequately described?						
Is the time for administration specified?						
Is the time needed for individuals to complete the survey given?						
Is the relevant literature included?						
Other?						

DESIGN AND SAMPLING	4	3	2	1	0	NA
Is the design described adequately?						
Is the design justified?						
If a sample, are sampling methods adequately described?						
If a sample, are the survey's participants randomly selected?						
If more than one group, are the survey's participants randomly assigned?						
If the unit that is sampled (e.g., students or employees) is not the population of main concern (e.g., teachers or managers), is this addressed in the report (e.g., in the analysis or discussion)?						
If a sample, and a nonrandom sampling method is used, is evidence given regarding the similarity of the groups at baseline?						
If groups are not equivalent at baseline, is this problem adequately addressed in the analysis or the interpretation?						
Are criteria given for including all sampling units (e.g., students, teachers) and whoever else is studied?						
Are criteria given for excluding units?						
Is the sample size justified, say, with a power calculation?						
Is information given on the number of participants in the source population?						

→

DESIGN AND SAMPLING	4	3	2	1	0	NA
Is information given on the number of participants eligible to participate?						
Is information given on the number who agreed to participate?						
Is information given on the number who refused to participate?						
Is information given on the number who dropped out or were lost to follow-up before completing the survey?						
Is information given on the number of respondents who completed all questions?						
Is information given on the number on whom some data are missing?						
If observations or measures are made over time, is the time period justified?						
Are reasons given for individuals or groups who dropped out?						
Are reasons given for missing data?						
Are the effects on generalizability of choice, equivalence, and participation of the resultant sample explained?						
Are the effects on internal validity of choice, equivalence, and participation of the resultant sample explained?						
Other?						

RELIABILITY AND VALIDITY	4	3	2	1	0	NA
Are the independent variables defined?						
Are the dependent variables defined?						
Are data provided on the survey's reliability for each variable?						
Are data provided on the survey's validity for each variable?						
Are the methods for ensuring reliability (e.g., quality assurance and training) described?						
Are the methods for ensuring reliability adequate?						
Are the methods for ensuring validity described?						
Are the methods for ensuring validity adequate?						
Are the scoring methods adequately described?						
Are the scaling methods described?						
Are the scaling methods adequate?						
Is the survey's administration adequately described?						
Is information provided on methods for ensuring the quality of data collection?						
Is the duration of the survey justified?						

→

RELIABILITY AND VALIDITY	4	3	2	1	0	NA
Is the duration sufficient for the survey's objectives?						
Are the effects on the survey's generalizability and practicality of the selection, reliability, validity of data sources, and the length of data collection explained?						
Other?						

DATA ANALYSIS	4	3	2	1	0	NA
Are statistical methods adequately described?						
Are statistical methods justified?						
Is the purpose of the analysis clear?						
Are scoring systems described?						
Are potential confounders adequately controlled for in the analysis?						
Are analytic specifications of the independent and dependent variables consistent with the survey's research questions or hypotheses?						
Is the unit of analysis specified clearly?						
Other?						

REPORTING	4	3	2	1	0	NA
Are references given for complex statistical methods?						
Are complex statistical methods described in an appendix?						
Are exact p values given?						
Are confidence intervals given?						
Are the results of the analysis clearly described?						
Are the survey's findings clearly described?						
Do the conclusions follow from the survey's results?						
Are the survey's limitations discussed adequately?						
Does the validity of the findings outweigh the limitations?						
Other?						

Exercises

1. Create a pie chart from the following information.

Thirty-four counties were surveyed about the actions they take after a mother tests positive for drugs and the child is referred to Child Protective Services. The findings are that 5% of the children received no services, 20% remained at home with informal supervision, dependency petitions were filed for 64%, and other actions taken for 11%.

2. Present the following information in a slide format. In so doing, include the percentage as well as the number of counties.

> Drug testing for women and infants was done under four conditions: mandatorily without mother's consent, tested with consent, anonymous testing, and other protocols. Of 28 counties that responded to the survey, 15 used mandatory testing, 10 only tested if mothers consented, 9 used other protocols, and 2 used anonymous testing. Some counties conducted tests under more than one condition.

3. Draw a bar chart, using the data in Table X below.

Table X
Major Causes of Adolescent Mortality, 1985
(10-19 years old)

Cause	% Mortality
Motor vehicle accidents	38
Natural causes	27
Suicide	10
Other vehicle/injury	10
Homicide	9
Drowning	4
Fires	2

SOURCE: "Trends and Current Status in Childhood Mortality: United States, 1900-1985," by L. Fingerhut and J. Kleinman, *Vital and Health Statistics,* Series 3, No. 26 (DHHS Publication No. 89-1410). Hyattsville, MD: National Center for Health Statistics, 1989.

4. Write the text for the table on page 54 in Chapter 2.

5. Write the text for Table Y, which shows the results of a survey of high school students' knowledge and beliefs especially as they pertain to welfare reform. A statistically significant result is $p < .05$.

Table Y
Baseline and Follow-up Mean, (*SD*),
and Net Change Scores for Outcomes,
by Treatment Group (*N* = 860 students)

Outcome	Experimental Group		Control Group		Net Difference	*t*	*p*
	Pre	Post	Pre	Post			
Knowledge	75.6 (11.6)	85.5 (8.8)	78.8 (10.9)	81.2 (9.6)	7.50	8.9	.0001
Attitude toward reform	2.5 (1.1)	2.1 (1.0)	2.5 (1.1)	2.3 (1.1)	−0.15	1.5	.14
Beliefs	3.5 (0.7)	3.8 (0.7)	3.7 (0.7)	3.8 (0.7)	0.19	4.7	.0001
Risk-taking behavior	4.4 (0.6)	4.5 (0.6)	4.4 (0.6)	4.4 (0.6)	0.09	1.2	.22
Values	5.4 (0.9)	5.5 (0.8)	5.5 (0.9)	5.5 (0.9)	0.09	0.7	.50
Self-efficacy	2.8 (0.6)	2.9 (0.6)	2.8 (0.6)	2.8 (0.6)	0.12	3.0	.003
Political preferences	3.7 (0.7)	3.9 (0.7)	3.8 (0.7)	3.8 (0.7)	0.10	2.2	.03
Religiosity	1.5 (0.5)	1.3 (2.3)	1.3 (2.4)	1.3 (2.4)	−0.48	2.8	.006

Answers

1.   Actions After Referral to Child Protective Services
     (*N* = 34 Counties)

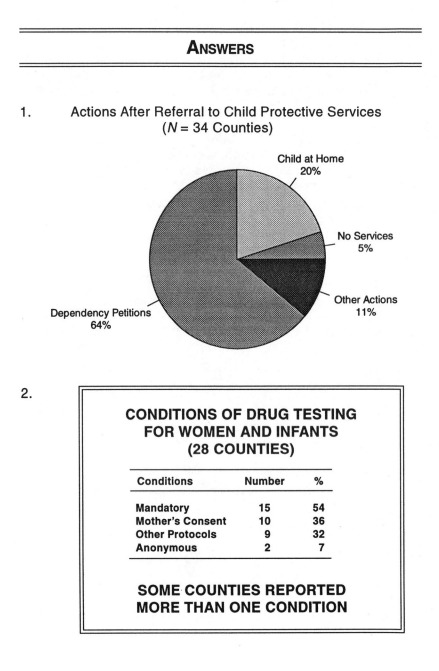

Child at Home
20%

No Services
5%

Other Actions
11%

Dependency Petitions
64%

2.

CONDITIONS OF DRUG TESTING FOR WOMEN AND INFANTS (28 COUNTIES)

Conditions	Number	%
Mandatory	15	54
Mother's Consent	10	36
Other Protocols	9	32
Anonymous	2	7

SOME COUNTIES REPORTED MORE THAN ONE CONDITION

3.

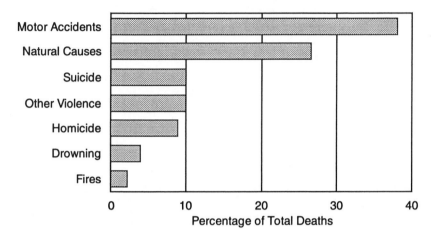

Major Causes of Adolescent Mortality—1985
(10-19 Years Old)

4. Table X compares dangers in the living room, hall, bedroom, and kitchen. The survey found that the living room and hallway areas of the experimental homes were signficantly less likely to have tripping dangers from loose floor coverings and peeling paint than were the same areas in control homes. The differences were smaller in the experimental and control homes for the bedrooms, and no statistically meaningful differences were obtained between both groups for the kitchen.

5. Table Y presents the pre- and postsurvey means and observed net change scores for each of eight outcomes for 860 students. Significant effects favoring the experiment were observed for five (knowledge, beliefs, self-efficacy, political preferences, and religiosity) of the eight outcomes.

Suggested Readings

Bailar, J. C., & Mosteller, F. (1988). Guidelines for statistical reporting in articles for medical journals. *Annals of Internal Medicine, 108,* 266-273.

The title of this article suggests that it is primarily appropriate for articles in medical journals. However, others can benefit from the discussion on figures and tables and the merits of confidence intervals and exact p values.

Bates, E. S., & Abemayor, E. (1991). Slide presentation graphics using a personal computer. *Archives of Otolaryngology and Head and Neck Surgery, 117,* 1026-1030.

An evaluation of four graphics programs for making slides. Although out of date in terms of technology and cost, the criteria used by the authors are still relevant.

Fink, A. (1993). *Evaluation fundamentals: Guiding health programs, research, and policy.* Newbury Park, CA: Sage.

This book devotes a chapter to written and oral reports. Examples are given of complete reports, executive summaries, and abstracts.

Lin, Y.-C. (1989). Practical approaches to scientific presentation. *Chinese Journal of Physiology, 32,* 71-78.

Describes the purposes, language, and style of oral presentation, with particular emphasis on using slides in scientific presentations.

Pfeiffer, W. S. (1991). *Technical writing.* New York: Macmillan.

Provides useful tips on the details of putting together formal reports. Discusses the cover and title page, table of contents, and executive summary. It also contains rules for preparing charts and giving oral presentations. Its orientation is for business, but many of the lessons can be adapted to health evaluation.

Spinler, S. (1991). How to prepare and deliver pharmacy presentations. *American Journal of Hospital Pharmacy, 48,* 1730-1738.

Provides extremely useful tips on the preparation and use of slides. Also discusses how to rehearse and then deliver an oral presentation.

About the Author

ARLENE FINK, PhD, is Professor of Medicine and Public Health at the University of California, Los Angeles. She is on the Policy Advisory Board of UCLA's Robert Wood Johnson Clinical Scholars Program, a health research scientist at the Veterans Administration Medical Center in Sepulveda, California, and president of Arlene Fink Associates. She has conducted evaluations throughout the United States and abroad and has trained thousands of health professionals, social scientists, and educators in program evaluation. Her published works include nearly 100 monographs and articles on evaluation methods and research. She is coauthor of *How to Conduct Surveys* and author of *Evaluation Fundamentals: Guiding Health Programs, Research, and Policy* and *Evaluation for Education and Psychology.*